Presented to: _My friend_

From: _Jane_

Who is wise and understanding among you?
Let him show it by his good life, by deeds done in the
humility that comes from wisdom.

JAMES 3:1

Bible Promises for Men
Copyright 1998 by the Zondervan Corporation

ISBN: 0-310-97691-X

Excerpts taken from: *The Men's Devotional Bible: New International Version*
Copyright 1993 by the Zondervan Corporation
All rights reserved.

The Holy Bible: New International Version Copyright 1973, 1978, 1984 by International Bible Society
"NIV" and "New International Version" trademarks are registered in the United States Patent and Trademark
Office by International Bible Society.

Requests for information should be addressed to:

ZondervanPublishingHouse
Mail Drop B20
Grand Rapids, Michigan 49530
http://www.zondervan.com

Senior Editor: Gwen Ellis
Compiler: Candy Paull
Design: Mark Veldheer

Printed in the United States of America
98 99 00 01 /DP/ 8 7 6 5 4 3 2 1

But as for me, I watch in hope for the LORD, I wait for God my Savior; my God will hear me.

MICAH 7:7

God is looking for an opportunity to reveal himself to you, so if you put him to the test and then watch for an answer without too many preconceptions about how that answer will come, I can guarantee you that you'll be in for some exciting surprises.

—PAT BOONE

I'm part of the fellowship of the unashamed. I have the Holy Spirit power. I have stepped over the line. The decision has been made—I'm a disciple of his. I won't look back, let up, slow down, back away, or be still. My past is redeemed, my present makes sense, my future is secure.

—A YOUNG PASTOR IN ZIMBABWE, AFRICA,
LATER MARTYRED FOR HIS FAITH IN CHRIST.

Do not be anxious about anything,
but in everything, by prayer and
petition, with thanksgiving, present
your requests to God.

PHILIPPIANS 4:6

Paul does not deny that the worst things will happen finally to all of us. He does not try to explain them away as God's will or God's judgment or God's method of testing our spiritual fiber. He simply tells the Philippians they are to keep in constant touch with the One who unimaginably transcends the worst things as he also unimaginably transcends the best.

—FREDERICK BUECHNER

Does your problem seem bigger than life, bigger than God himself? It isn't. God is infinitely bigger than any problem you ever had or will have, and every time you call a problem unsolvable, you mock God. "With God all things are possible."

—BILL HYBELS

*Jesus looked at them and said,
"With man this is impossible, but with
God all things are possible."*

MATTHEW 19:26

I have learned that when God looks upon his Body, spread like an archipelago throughout the world, he sees the whole thing. And I think he, understanding the cultural backgrounds and true intent of the worshipers, likes the variety he sees.

—PAUL BRAND

And God said to him, "I am God Almighty;
be fruitful and increase in number. A nation
and a community of nations will come from you,
and kings will come from your body."

GENESIS 35:11

Redemption in Jesus Christ initiates a new life, one in which the life of God invades ours, making the passage of time take on the significance of eternity.

—WILLIAM T. MCCONNELL

But do not forget this one thing, dear friends: With the Lord a day is like a thousand years, and a thousand years are like a day.

2 PETER 3:8

A generous man will prosper; he who refreshes others will himself be refreshed.

PROVERBS 11:25

God has made us to be givers. It isn't something we have to do in order to please him so much as it's something we need to do to keep ourselves working properly. We are healthy and whole when we are both giving and receiving.

—Daniel Taylor

*F*rom him the whole body, joined and held together
by every supporting ligament, grows and builds
itself up in love, as each part does its work.

EPHESIANS 4:16

The Body of Christ, like our own bodies, is composed of individual, unlike cells that are knit together to form one Body. He is the whole thing, and the joy of the Body increases as individual cells realize they can be diverse without becoming isolated outposts.

—PAUL BRAND

The contest for America's moral leadership is still going on; whether the church is willing and able to step up to its Biblical responsibility is still to be decided. It may be the greatest question we face.

—CHARLES COLSON

To each of his disciples, Jesus simply said, "Follow me." That was an invitation, not a requirement. An invitation respects the freedom of the invitee to accept or decline. Indeed, the "no" answer is perhaps the greatest expression of human dignity possible.

—JOHN FISCHER

Let the peace of Christ rule in your hearts, since as members of one body you were called to peace. And be thankful.

The magic of a thankful spirit is that it has the power to replace anger with love, resentment with happiness, fear with faith, worry with peace, and the desire to dominate with the wish to play on a team.

—DONALD E. DEMARAY

The Lord is gracious and compassionate, slow to anger and rich in love.

God's ways are not our ways. We are so selfish. He is so self-giving, so self-sharing! We are so short-tempered. He is so patient, so persevering! We are so hard and critical. He is so merciful and kind.

—W. Phillip Keller

Without the burden of past mistakes or anxiety about failing in the future, I'm free to concentrate on doing my very best in the present. And I believe that's how real, personal Christian faith can make it easier for anyone to reach his or her highest potential.

—TOM LANDRY

Let the wicked forsake his way and the evil man his thoughts. Let him turn to the LORD, and he will have mercy on him, and to our God, for he will freely pardon.

ISAIAH 55:7

In our rating-conscious society that ranks everything from baseball teams to "the best chili in New York," an attitude of relative worth can easily seep into the church of Christ. The church Jesus founded is much more like a family in which the son, retarded from birth, has as much worth as his brother, the Rhodes scholar.

—PAUL BRAND

In your life you should always have some people whom you nourish and who return little or nothing to you. You should also have people who nourish you, but you may return nothing to them. A third kind of relationship is equal sharing. This is friendship.

—JIM CONWAY

"You asked, 'Who is this that obscures my counsel without knowledge?' Surely I spoke of things I did not understand, things too wonderful for me to know."

JOB 42:3

God does not reveal his plan, he reveals himself. He comes to us as warmth when we are cold, fellowship when we are alone, strength when we are weak, peace when we are troubled, courage when we are afraid, songs when we are sad, and bread when we are hungry.

—Bob Benson

But just as you excel in everything—in faith, in speech, in knowledge, in complete earnestness and in your love for us—see that you also excel in this grace of giving.

2 Corinthians 8:7

Giving is to your benefit. It doesn't make you a saint or a martyr to give. In giving you are simply reflecting God's image—he who gave everything. Miserliness in all forms—monetary and emotional—diminishes us. The more we keep the less we have. And the less we are. This is one of life's interesting paradoxes.

—DANIEL TAYLOR

Work in a normal, healthy human context, work with a sane and moderate human measure, integrated in a productive social milieu, is by itself capable of contributing much to the spiritual life.

—THOMAS MERTON

*F*inally, brothers, whatever is true, whatever is noble, whatever is right, whatever is pure, whatever is lovely, whatever is admirable—if anything is excellent or praiseworthy—think about such things.

PHILIPPIANS 4:8

May the favor of the Lord our
God rest upon us; establish the work of
our hands for us—yes, establish the
work of our hands.

PSALM 90:17

Men can dignify labor by doing ordinary things, but as redeemed persons. There lies the difference, and this is where the drudgery dissipates—God is in it. That means that every work bench in a plant is an altar! So you see, we can please the Lord by our work.

—TED ENGSTROM AND DAVID JUROE

*All you have made will
praise you, O LORD;
your saints will extol you.*

PSALM 145:10

Father, we are thankful for the reminders you give us daily in the form of our children. Reminders, first, of your generosity, for children are a gift from you. But reminders, as well, of our finitude, or our place in this world that you have created.

—S.D. GAEDE

O Divine Master, grant that I may not so much seek to be consoled as to console; to be understood as to understand; to be loved as to love; for it is in giving that we receive; it is in pardoning that we are pardoned; and it is in dying that we are born to Eternal Life.

—Francis of Assisi

Who is wise and understanding among you? Let him show it by his good life, by deeds done in the humility that comes from wisdom.

JAMES 3:13

*A*fter six days Jesus took Peter,
James and John with him and led them up
a high mountain, where they were all alone.
There he was transfigured before them.

MARK 9:2

You don't need to be a friend to everyone. Remember the model of Jesus. He preached to, ministered to, and healed thousands of people, but he only had twelve disciples. Of those twelve, only three were invited with him when he was transfigured on the mountain.

—JIM CONWAY

It's one thing to reach out to a needy person, but it's another to have a friendship. In the first situation you're doing social work or a spiritual ministry of caring. When you are truly a friend, you and your friend will be giving equally to each other.

—JIM CONWAY

One thing I ask of the LORD, this is what I seek: that I may dwell in the house of the LORD all the days of my life, to gaze upon the beauty of the LORD and to seek him in his temple.

PSALM 27:4

Help me to understand that only a few things really are necessary in life. And when you get right down to it, only one: to sit at your feet ... listening ... looking into your eyes ... and loving you.

—KEN GIRE

No matter how sound my strategy, how much I study, how hard I work—I'll always be a failure when it comes to being perfect. Yet God loves me anyway. And believing that gives me the greatest sense of peace, calm and security in the world.

—TOM LANDRY

Christ came to give us a sense of calling in everyday work. This is where the world is changed, and where the kingdom is built.

—BRUCE LARSON

As for man, his days are like grass, he flourishes like a flower of the field; the wind blows over it and it is gone, and its place remembers it no more.

PSALM 103:15

Stop and consider the brevity of our years on earth, perhaps finding new motivation to preserve the values that will endure. Why should we work ourselves into an early grave, missing those precious moments with loved ones who crave our affection and attention?

—JAMES DOBSON

If you love me, you will obey
what I command.

John 14:15

The commandment of Jesus is not a sort of spiritual shock treatment. Jesus asks nothing of us without giving us the strength to perform it. His commandment never seeks to destroy life, but to foster, strengthen and heal it.

—DIETRICH BONHOEFFER

There is a striking difference between knowing about God and knowing God. We may know the right God-words yet not experience God. Only in Jesus, the Son of God, can we truly know God the Father.

—REUBEN R. WELCH

*T*he man who says, "I know him," but does not do what he commands is a liar, and the truth is not in him.

1 JOHN 2:4

"In the same way, on the outside you appear to people as righteous but on the inside you are full of hypocrisy and wickedness."

MATTHEW 23:28

You and I as Christians need to realize that however acceptable our lives may be for the general audience, we still possess an R-rated heart, and we're as good as dead if we want God to meet us on any other ground than his grace and forgiveness.

—JOHN FISCHER

Religion that God our Father accepts as pure and faultless is this: to look after orphans and widows in their distress and to keep oneself from being polluted by the world.

JAMES 1:27

The clear duty of real men goes beyond "live and let live." We are mandated to protect widows, orphans, the alien and all those who lack sustaining relationships. As long as men and boys fail to be protective, they will fall prey to the typical male sexual fantasy that sells [pornographic] magazines and films.

—E. JAMES WILDER

As we stand before God, we are
judged on the basis of Christ's perfection,
not our own unworthiness.

—PAUL BRAND

*T*herefore, if anyone is in Christ,
he is a new creation; the old has gone,
the new has come!

2 CORINTHIANS 5:17

For it is written: "Be holy, because I am holy."

1 PETER 1:16

The saint seeks not his own glory but the glory of God. And in order that God may be glorified in all things, the saint wishes himself to be nothing but a pure instrument of the divine will. He wants himself to be simply a window through which God's mercy shines on the world. And for this he strives to be holy.

—THOMAS MERTON

Be devoted to one another in brotherly love. Honor one another above yourselves.

❖

ROMANS 12:10

Like genuine love, honor is a gift we give to someone. It involves the decision we make before we put love into action that a person is of high value. In fact, love for someone often begins to flow once we have made the decision to honor him.

—GARY SMALLEY AND JOHN TRENT

"*Just as the Son of Man did not come to be served, but to serve, and to give his life as a ransom for many.*"

MATTHEW 20:28

The long painful history of the church is the history of people ever and again tempted to choose power over love, control over the cross, being a leader over being led. Those who resisted this temptation to the end, and thereby give us hope, are the true saints.

—HENRI NOUWEN

Fathers who are honest with themselves will admit that we all make mistakes. We have all made bad decisions. Some of those decisions have to be reversed.

—MIKE SINGLETARY

Blessed is the man who makes the LORD his trust, who does not look to the proud, to those who turn aside to false gods.

PSALM 40:4

*H*as not the LORD made them one? In flesh and spirit they are his. And why one? Because he was seeking godly offspring. So guard yourself in your spirit, and do not break faith with the wife of your youth.

MALACHI 2:15

If you will honor God by being obedient, he will honor you by throwing you some kind of banquet. I can't tell you how, I can't tell you when, but I can tell you that he keeps his word. He is the God of surprises, and if you remain faithful in that tough marriage, he will surprise you one day with joy.

—STEVE FARRAR

With this authority a husband can pray against the dark forces he may feel pressing in on him and his family. He prays this way against sickness, against temptations, against forces in his community that would corrupt his children.

—LEONARD LESOURD

*T*he weapons we fight with are not the weapons of the world. On the contrary, they have divine power to demolish strongholds.

2 CORINTHIANS 10:4

And over all these virtues put on love, which binds them all together in perfect unity.

COLOSSIANS 3:14

Love that is at liberty to be realistic calls us to recognize that marriage is something that must be worked out. The art of marriage, it has been said, is in maintaining equilibrium through the various changes and adjustments of life together.

—G.R. SLATER

God's not the Cosmic Bookkeeper, the one to blame if things don't work out the way you think they should. Life isn't always fair, at least in the short run, but the Bible taught me not to confuse life with God. When you're confronted with trouble you ask God, "What do you want me to do in this situation?"

—DAVE DRAVECKY

True faith depends not upon mysterious signs, celestial fireworks, or grandiose dispensations from a God who is seen as a rich, benevolent uncle; true faith, as Job understood, rests on the assurance that *God is who he is*. Indeed, on that we must be willing to stake our very lives.

—CHARLES COLSON

You have stolen my heart, my sister, my bride;
you have stolen my heart with one glance of your
eyes, with one jewel of your necklace.

SONG OF SONGS 4:9

Sometimes I look at Sandy sleeping, unaware of me, vulnerable as a child, and remember that she lived a good part of her life before I even entered it. This woman is my wife. She surprises me, and I am glad for that because it renews our marriage.

—RODNEY CLAPP

It is not objective proof of God's existence that we want but the experience of God's presence. That is the miracle we are really after, and that is also, I think, the miracle that we really get.

—FREDERICK BUECHNER

*The Word became flesh and made his dwelling
among us. We have seen his glory, the glory
of the One and Only, who came from the Father,
full of grace and truth.*

JOHN 1:14

The earth is the LORD's,
and everything in it, the world,
and all who live in it.

PSALM 24:1

The Lord didn't create the earth and then abandon it. He is intimately involved with sustaining it. He watches over what belongs to him.

—DON WYRTZEN

*T*herefore, since we are receiving a kingdom that cannot be shaken, let us be thankful, and so worship God acceptably with reverence and awe.

HEBREWS 12:28

In our day we must begin to recover a sense of awe and profound reverence for God. We must begin to view him once again in the infinite majesty that alone belongs to him who is the Creator and Supreme Ruler of the entire universe.

—JERRY BRIDGES

"I will remain in the world no longer, but they are still in the world, and I am coming to you. Holy Father, protect them by the power of your name—the name you gave me—so that they may be one as we are one."

JOHN 17:11

I must admit that most of my worship in the last thirty years has not taken place among people who have shared my taste in music, speech, or even thought. But over those years I have been profoundly—and humbly—impressed that I find God in the faces of my fellow worshipers.

—PAUL BRAND

We believe that the death of Christ is just that point in history at which something absolutely unimaginable from outside shows through into our own world.

—C.S. Lewis

After 10 years in a Soviet gulag, Alexander Solzhenitsyn wrote "Bless you, prison, for having been in my life." For it was there he learned that "the meaning of earthly existence lies, not as we have grown used to thinking, in prospering, but in the development of the soul."

—CHARLES COLSON

What, then, shall we say in response to this? If God is for us, who can be against us?

ROMANS 8:31

God is on our side, right or wrong, because even when we are wrong, he still loves us.

—MICHAEL CARD

Growing up, I had always been at the center of attention. That kind of motivation can keep you going strong, so long as you succeed. But it's not so good for dealing with failure. Seeing Jesus Christ as your audience shifts the pressure off yourself. You do your best to bring glory to God, not yourself. If you lose, the loss will hurt, but God will still be there.

—DAVE DRAVECKY

So we say with confidence,
"The Lord is my helper, I will not be afraid.
What can man do to me?"

HEBREWS 13:6

*But just as he who called you is holy,
so be holy in all you do.*

1 PETER 1:15

Let us not delude ourselves with easy and infantile conceptions of holiness. Mere external respectability, without deeper or more positive moral values, brings discredit upon the Christian faith.

—Thomas Merton

Sitting down, Jesus called the Twelve and said, "If anyone wants to be first, he must be the very last, and the servant of all."

MARK 9:35

A home is filled with fragrant and appealing spiritual riches when each member adopts a servant's spirit. A person filled with the Spirit of Christ strongly desires to serve. He does not seek to establish his own emotional turf but freely edifies and encourages other family members through his servant spirit.

—CHARLES STANLEY

He must manage his own family well and see that his children obey him with proper respect.

1 TIMOTHY 3:4

The spirit of rebellion has come about because children have never learned respect for authority as their parents did not exercise authority; on the other hand, it is also possible that they did not learn respect for authority because the parents misused it. Authority must never be exercised in an arbitrary, unreasonable manner.

—J.H. WATERINK

We cannot delegate our Christian love and compassion and concern in every instance to a paid professional or functionary. We are enjoined to love our neighbor—not just to pay taxes to employ someone else to love our neighbor.

—JOHN B. ANDERSON

"*Is not this the kind of fasting I have chosen: to loose the chains of injustice and untie the cords of the yoke, to set the oppressed free and break every yoke?*"

ISAIAH 58:6

The better we are at seeing through trials to what they can produce in our lives and our children's lives, the better able we'll be to provide calmness, assurance and genuine love to our children, even in the midst of trying times.

—GARY SMALLEY AND JOHN TRENT

*Consider it pure joy,
my brothers, whenever you face
trials of many kinds.*

JAMES 1:2

Train a child in the way he should go, and when he is old he will not turn from it.

PROVERBS 22:6

In Proverbs 22:6, the word *way* is used in this sense: "train up a child in keeping with his characteristics." And his characteristics are distinct and set. There is a bent already established within every child God places in our care.

—CHARLES SWINDOLL

But you are a chosen people, a royal priesthood, a holy nation, a people belonging to God, that you may declare the praises of him who called you out of darkness into his wonderful light.

1 Peter 2:9

Let what you do arise out of who you are. Being is more important than doing. I have decided that whatever I do for the rest of my life will be the result of allowing my God-given self to emerge. I'm done with posturing for a public that demands an unattainable and hypocritical perfection.

—Stan Mooneyham

We can speak of a man's choosing his vocation, but perhaps it is at least as accurate to speak of a vocation's choosing the man, of a call's being given and a man's hearing it, or not hearing it. What kind of voice do we listen for?

—FREDERICK BUECHNER

With this in mind, we constantly pray for you, that our God may count you worthy of his calling, and that by his power he may fulfill every good purpose of yours and every act prompted by your faith.

2 THESSALONIANS 1:11

Until the evil man finds evil unmistakably present in his existence, in the form of pain, he is enclosed in illusion. No doubt Pain as God's megaphone is a terrible instrument; but it gives the only opportunity the bad man can have for amendment. It plants the flag of truth within the fortress of a rebel soul.

—C.S. LEWIS

M y *dear brothers, take note of this:*
Everyone should be quick to listen, slow to
speak and slow to become angry.

JAMES 1:19

Someone once described the contrast between a good life and a godly life as the difference between the top of the ocean and the bottom. On the top, sometimes it's like glass, and other times it's raging and stormy. But hundreds of fathoms below, it is beautiful and consistent, always calm, always peaceful.

—BILL MCCARTNEY

What makes the temptation of power so seemingly irresistible? Maybe it is that power offers an easy substitute for the hard task of love. It seems easier to be God than to love God, easier to control people than to love people, easier to own life than to love life.

—HENRI NOUWEN

"I looked for a man among them who would build up the wall and stand before me in the gap on behalf of the land so I would not have to destroy it, but I found none."

In this desperately crucial, convulsive time, *unavailability is a terrible sin*. The times demand big men. Not men who are big shots (they're useless), but men who are big in heart and mind. Large-souled men! *Men with a vision*—whose feet are on the ground but whose eyes are on the far horizon. Farsighted, selfless men. *Men with a goal!* Men committed—*dedicated to God* and his holy, high purposes! Men of integrity!

—Richard Halverson

He raises the poor from the dust and lifts the needy from the ash heap; he seats them with princes and has them inherit a throne of honor. "For the foundations of the earth are the LORD's; upon them he has set the world."

1 SAMUEL 2:8

The person who thinks money is the measure of success suffers from a kind of poverty of the imagination and intellect as well as of the spirit. Others suffer a kind of poverty of the emotions, unable to intertwine their lives affirmingly with the lives of others. God offers us all of creation and a relationship with him. We have only our brokenness to offer back. (Thankfully, that is all that he requires.)

—DANIEL TAYLOR

In every bad relationship, self-centeredness is the deadliest culprit. Poor communication, temper problems, unhealthy responses to dysfunctional family backgrounds, codependent relationships, and personal incompatibility—everything (unless medically caused) flows out of the cesspool of self-centeredness.

—LARRY CRABB

But the wisdom that comes from heaven is first of all pure; then peace-loving, considerate, submissive, full of mercy and good fruit, impartial and sincere.

JAMES 3:17

"Ask and it will be given to you; seek and you will find; knock and the door will be opened to you."

MATTHEW 7:7

Just as surely as we are looking in different ways, answers are coming to us in a diversity which reflects the mystery of God himself. The wonderful thing is that he is making certain we are receiving and that we are finding and that doors are being opened to us.

—BOB BENSON

Is money the root of all evil? No. The love of money is. But we shouldn't rest too easily because of that distinction. We show what we love by that to which we most happily devote our attention.

—DANIEL TAYLOR

*F*or the love of money is a root of all kinds of evil.
Some people, eager for money, have wandered from
the faith and pierced themselves with many griefs.

1 TIMOTHY 6:10

He has made everything beautiful in its time. He has also set eternity in the hearts of men; yet they cannot fathom what God has done from beginning to end.

ECCLESIASTES 3:11

*F*or God did not give us a spirit of timidity, but a spirit of power, of love and of self-discipline.

2 TIMOTHY 1:7

God would be within his rights to either ignore our attempts at control or simply push us and our petty little pretensions aside. But thanks be to God, he is not like that. Instead, out of his grace and mercy he reminds us of the folly of our ways. And one way he has done this in my life is through my children.

—S.D. GAEDE

No wonder the Creator made marriage permanent—after a lifetime we have only just begun to understand the marvelous inner clockwork of each other.

—RICHARD FOSTER

But those who hope in the LORD *will renew their strength. They will soar on wings like eagles; they will run and not grow weary, they will walk and not be faint.*

ISAIAH 40:31

It was Jesus himself who reminded us that we were to call him Father—"Abba Father"—which is a lot more like calling him Dad. I think Jesus was telling us that our Father is the one in the stands who is standing on the seat, waving his coat in a circle over his head, with tears of pride and happiness running down his face.

—BOB BENSON

God is with us on our journeys. He is there when we are home. He sits with us at our table. He knows about funerals and weddings and commencements and hospitals and jails and unemployment and labor and laughter and rest and tears. He knows because he is with us. He comes to us again and again.

—BOB BENSON

The spiritual life is not a life of quiet withdrawal, a hothouse of growth of artificial ascetic practices beyond the reach of people living ordinary lives. It is in the ordinary duties and labors of life that the Christian can and should develop his spiritual union with God.

—THOMAS MERTON

But the fruit of the Spirit is love, joy, peace, patience, kindness, goodness, faithfulness . . .

GALATIANS 5:22

Our goal is balance . . . always balance. Not either-or, but both-and. Not just *tough*. That alone makes a man cold, distant, intolerant, unbearable. But tough *and* tender . . . gentle, thoughtful, teachable, considerate.

—CHARLES SWINDOLL

The true saint is not one who has become convinced that he himself is holy, but one who is overwhelmed by the realization that God, and God alone, is holy.

—THOMAS MERTON

Giving and gratitude go together like humor and laughter, like having one's back rubbed and the sigh that follows, like a blowing wind and the murmur of wind chimes. Gratitude keeps alive the rhythm of grace given and grace grateful, a lively lilt that lightens a heavy world.

—LEWIS B. SMEDES

"*I will betroth you to me forever; I will betroth you in righteousness and justice, in love and compassion.*"

HOSEA 2:19

It takes three to get married—a man, a woman and God. Francis de Sales put it this way, "If the glue is good, two pieces of wood glued together will cleave so fast to each other that they can be more easily broken in any other place than where they were joined. God glued the husband to the wife with his own blood."

—G.R. Slater

Marriage is a stage on which real love—the kind the apostle Paul described as the greatest virtue—can be enacted for the world to see: the kind of love that enables us to endure wrong with patience, to resist evil with conviction, to enjoy the good things with gusto, to give richly of ourselves with humility, and to nourish another's soul with long-suffering.

—LARRY CRABB

Love is patient, love is kind.
It does not envy, it does not boast,
it is not proud.

1 CORINTHIANS 13:4

We don't have to explain miracles;
all we have to do is accept them.

—Ben Carson

God wants to be loved as a father and mother are loved by their children, as a friend by a friend, as a man by his wife and a wife by her husband, as a sick person by a caring nurse and as a guest by his host. God finds great joy when we express our feelings toward him.

—WALTER TROBISH

*T*hey exchanged the truth of God for a lie, and worshiped and served created things rather than the Creator—who is forever praised. Amen.

ROMANS 1:25

We want Christianity to work. We want it to exist in a closed system where every question has an answer, every problem has a solution. We want to show the world a neat, clean, open-and-shut case for Christianity. But in the process, we unknowingly shut out God. Claiming to be wise, we become fools; we exchange the truth of God for a lie.

—JOHN FISCHER

As for God, his way is perfect;
the word of the LORD is flawless. He is a
shield for all who take refuge in him.

2 SAMUEL 22:31

The longing of all mankind is to have security. God created man and then he created a place for him, the Garden of Eden. When man lost God, he lost at the same time his place. Since then, the longing for a place where he belongs, is in the heart of every human being. In light of this, Jesus' promise "to prepare a place" for us is filled with new meaning (John 14:2). Those who have found him have found their place.

—WALTER TROBISCH

Praying means to stop expecting from God that same small-mindedness which you discover in yourself. To pray is to walk in the full light of God, and to say simply, without holding back, "I am a man and you are God."

—HENRI NOUWEN

How is it to be explained—the very heart and mystery of the Christian faith? To soothe those battered old heads, to grasp those poor [leprous] stumps, to take in one's arms those children consigned to dustbins, because it is his head, as they are his stumps and his children, of whom he said that whosoever received one such child in his name received him.

—MALCOLM MUGGERIDGE

Let us not become weary in doing good, for at the proper time we will reap a harvest if we do not give up.

❧••❧

GALATIANS 6:9

Despair, which descends by dungeon steps to depression, is one of the major afflictions in our society. The besetting temptation of the life of the Spirit is simply to quit.

—Eugene H. Peterson

"*I* am the vine; you are the branches. If a man remains in me and I in him, he will bear much fruit; apart from me you can do nothing."

JOHN 15:5

Authentic, lasting significance is hid with Christ . . . That is to say, a man cannot find significance in any lasting way apart from Christ. So, if a man is in Christ, and submitted to God's plan and purpose, then he can satisfy his greatest need in a way that endures.

—PATRICK MORELY

When life caves in, you do not need reasons, you need comfort. You do not need some answers, you need some*one*. And Jesus does not come to us with an explanation; he comes to us with his presence.

—BOB BENSON

May your unfailing love be my comfort, according to your promise to your servant.

PSALM 119:76

For he will command his angels concerning you to guard you in all your ways.

PSALM 91:11

Believers, look up—take courage. The angels are nearer than you think.

—BILLY GRAHAM

I know that everything God does will endure forever; nothing can be added to it and nothing taken from it. God does it so that men will revere him.

ECCLESIASTES 3:14

If we complain of time and take such joy in the seemingly timeless moment, it suggests that we were created for eternity. Not only are we harried by time, we seem unable, despite a thousand generations, to even get used to it. If that is so, it may appear as a proof, or at least a powerful suggestion, that eternity exists and is our home.

—SHELDON VANAUKEN

Why are you downcast, O my soul? Why so disturbed within me? Put your hope in God, for I will yet praise him, my Savior and my God.

PSALM 42:11